WORKING IN

HEALTH CARE AND WELLNESS

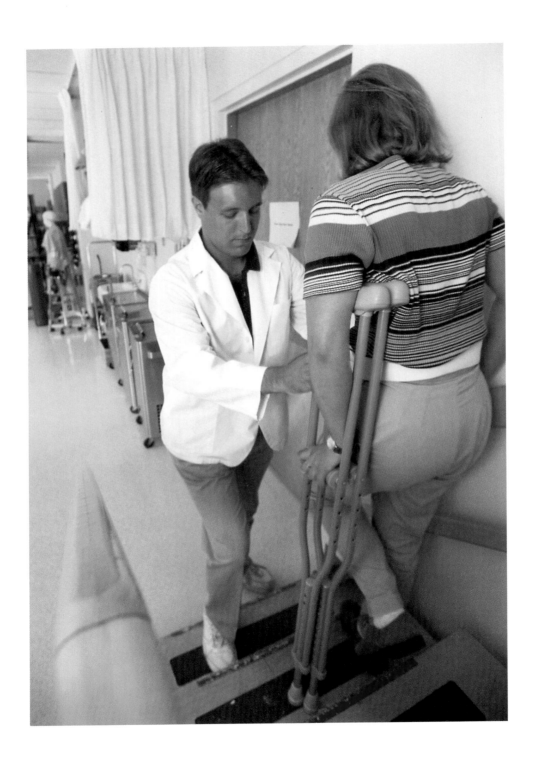

exploring careers

WORKING IN

HEALTH CARE AND WELLNESS

By Barbara Lee
Introduction by Barbara Sher

Lerner Publications Company • Minneapolis

For Ben, Molly, and Timothy

Acknowledgments

My thanks to the dozen people profiled in this book, who freely gave me hours of their time. And thanks also to the many friends and strangers—too many to name here—who helped me find just the right people to interview.

The Exploring Careers series was developed by Barbara Lee.

Library of Congress Cataloging-in-Publication Data

Lee, Barbara, 1945 –
    Working in health care and wellness / by Barbara Lee ; introduction by Barbara Sher.
    p. cm. — (Exploring Careers)
    Includes index.
    Summary: Profiles of twelve people who have careers in health care and wellness, including a paramedic, pharmacist, nutritionist, and acupuncturist.
    ISBN 0-8225-1760-4 (alk. paper)
    1. Medicine —Vocational guidance — Juvenile literature.
    [1. Medicine —Vocational guidance.] I. Title. II. Series:
    Exploring careers (Minneapolis, Minn.)
    R690.L396 1996
    610.69 — dc20   95-49876

Manufactured in the United States of America
1 2 3 4 5 6 – JR – 01 00 99 98 97 96

CONTENTS

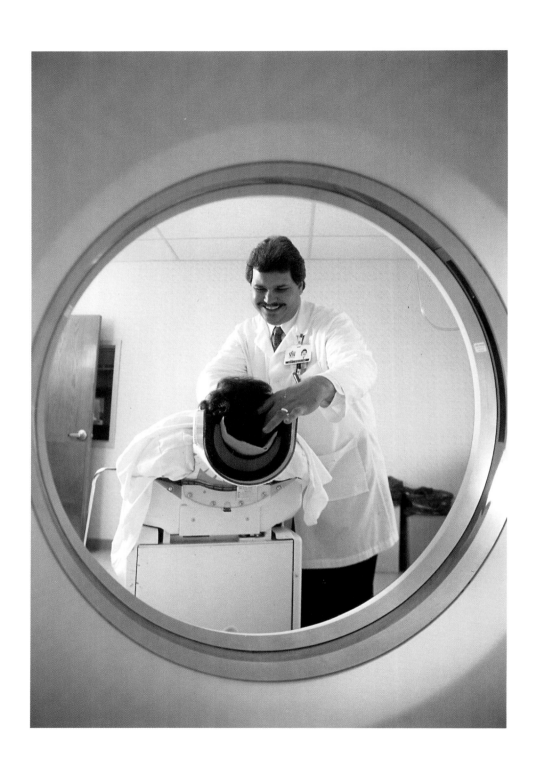

INTRODUCTION

by Barbara Sher

Welcome to the world of work. It's a remarkable world, filled with opportunities, almost too big to understand. There are indoor jobs and outdoor jobs. There are jobs that involve other people and jobs that don't. There are jobs you've never heard of and jobs with names you can't pronounce. And to complicate matters even more, the jobs of tomorrow may not be the same as the jobs of today.

But some things will remain the same. In fact, let me tell you a secret. For successful people, work is like play. That's right—play. That's because they've found the work that is best suited to who they are. Their careers fit their unique talents, their interests, and their skills and education.

Introduction

Begin by asking yourself what you love doing. What is fun? What makes you excited? The answers will give you some clues about what kind of work you might enjoy—and be good at. It's not too early to begin exploring. Talk to your teachers and parents, your friends and neighbors. Ask them to introduce you to people doing work that you would like to find out more about. You will be surprised by how willing people are to talk about what they do. Perhaps they will even show you around their workplaces.

Reading this book is a great start. Without leaving your chair, you will go to work with people who will tell you about what they do and why they do it. They will give you ideas.

Dr. Carolyn Hildreth, a physician, has chosen a career that fits her talents, interests, and personality.

Maybe their jobs will seem boring or hard. Or maybe they'll excite you. It doesn't matter. It's all part of exploring.

So let yourself be curious. Be a detective. Remember, you don't have to make up your mind right now. You are just collecting information. Good luck. And have fun!

Twelve Careers in Health Care and Wellness

f there's a field that's changing faster than fast, it's health care. High-tech equipment, sophisticated procedures, and new drugs save lives every day. Scientists are on the edge of breakthroughs that only a few years ago were the stuff of science fiction. Each month or two, biotechnologists learn about new genes, the very building blocks of life. Their discoveries may lead to early diagnosis and even prevention of diseases such as breast cancer.

At the same time that these medical breakthroughs have captured our attention, so have natural or "alternative" healing methods. Some of these systems of medicine have been used for hundreds, even thousands, of years. Many emphasize the prevention of illness or disease in addition to treatment. Practitioners of alternative medicine believe that the body has its own healing powers. They also believe it's important to treat the whole patient, not just the disease.

Health care is changing in another way. Most health professionals—both traditional and alternative—expect their patients to become active partners in the healing process. They may ask patients to eat a healthier diet, exercise more, and reduce their stress level by using techniques such as meditation.

The number of careers in health care is growing. Few people have the time, money, and dedication it takes to become a physician—four years of college, another four years in medical school, and years of training as an intern and resident. But there are many other possibilities. Some jobs are traditional and some are more unusual. Behind the scenes—and sometimes right up front—are dozens of health careers that might be right for you.

In the pages that follow, 12 people take you into their workaday worlds. Their stories shed light on what it takes to become a paramedic or a pharmacist, a nutritionist or an acupuncturist. Although most of these people hold advanced college degrees, experience and personal commitment also count. A few have known from an early age what they wanted to do. Others developed their interests over time. Each person is different.

As you read about careers in health care and

wellness, you will notice some similarities in all the stories. One is the way government policies directly affect the health care field. These policies regulate insurance companies, which pay the bills for most people when they are sick. Some Americans get their insurance from government programs such as Medicare. Others are covered by private insurance plans, paid for by individuals or their employers. Because of the complex system of insurance in the United States, all health care professionals have to handle massive amounts of paperwork.

Government agencies also determine who is qualified to provide health care. Most health care providers must pass difficult written and practical (hands-on) tests. They must also be licensed in their state.

The 12 people whose stories follow have diverse backgrounds, interests, and training. Underlying the success of each person are many years of education and hard work. The people profiled have developed a variety of skills and a knack for what they do. And if the perfect job didn't come along at first, some changed directions or learned new skills or volunteered their time. All of them want to help others.

Each of these 12 people will tell you what they like and don't like about their jobs. They all work in the mid-Atlantic region, but similar jobs can be found throughout the United States and Canada. Although no one can predict the future, everyone profiled in this book has an opinion about how his or her job will change in the future.

Twelve people. Twelve careers. Their stories may surprise you.

John Simone

Chapter One

PARAMEDIC

aramedic John Simone remembers the first baby he delivered. "He shot out into my arms," he says. "They don't get any easier than that." John cleared the baby's airways and checked his pulse. "I really got a kick out of it," he says. "I was invited to the christening." He keeps the baby's picture in his car.

"Each call is a little different," John says, referring to the emergency calls he and other paramedics at the Baltimore County Fire Department receive. Calls come in through the 911 emergency phone number.

During a routine shift, John may find himself giving mouth-to-mouth resuscitation, stopping severe bleeding, or handling heart attacks. Or there may be no calls at all. Although 95 percent of all cases are not life threatening, paramedics must be ready to respond instantly to a range of injuries and other emergencies.

It's the perfect career for someone who is outgoing and adventurous but steady as a rock, John says. "You have to keep a level head and think clearly in a crisis."

Since paramedics are on call 24 hours a day, John works both days and nights, a schedule he's adjusted to. He works two days a week from 7:00 A.M. to 5:00 P.M., then two nights from 5:00 P.M. to 7:00 A.M. Then he has four days off. Even though the night shift is longer, the paramedics get about the same number of calls as during the day shift.

You have to keep a level head and think clearly in a crisis.

During a typical day shift, John signs in, then checks the drug supplies in the ambulance and the batteries that run the equipment. The paramedics who are going off duty brief him about the night's calls, whether or not equipment was left at the hospital, and how much oxygen is left on board the ambulance. John works with a partner, one of two other paramedics at his station.

Since John is part of the fire department, he helps the firefighters make breakfast and clean up. He then handles paperwork for restocking the ambulance. By late morning, if there are no calls, the paramedics may drive around, memorizing the streets in their district or learning the layouts of large buildings such as nursing homes or day care centers. It's all part of being ready. During long spells with no 911 calls, they relax and watch television.

The paramedics also share "blood and guts" stories. Having a sense of humor allows paramedics to blow off steam and relieve the stress that goes with the job. John has seen gruesome car accidents in which people have bled to death. "I don't like to see anyone die, but it happens every day," he says. Treating kids is the hardest for him. "One died on me. He had stopped breathing."

It also can be difficult to deal with the family and friends of victims. "They have a variety of reactions—mostly grief, mild hysteria, and tears," John says. "I try to have a few kind words, but there's not enough time to talk. Things happen fast and several things are going on at once." He also may need to ask about a victim's medical history and get permission for certain medical procedures. "I hate to be short, but the victim may require all my attention," he says.

And so the day goes by, sometimes busy and stressful, other times quiet and tedious. When John's shift ends, before he leaves he briefs the paramedics working the next shift. On night shifts, paramedics try to get a little sleep between calls.

Finding the Right Career

John grew up in Connecticut. After high school, he enlisted for part-time duty in the National Guard, training as a field artillery surveyor. Since he planned a career as a pilot, he enrolled in Embry-Riddle Aeronautical University in Florida but dropped out after

John Simone

Paramedics may cross-train in both emergency medicine and firefighting.

two years. "I didn't have the aptitude for it," he says. "It never came easy. I was always uncomfortable and on edge."

Returning to Connecticut, John worked at odd jobs and signed up for a class to become an emergency medical technician (EMT). The course required classroom and clinical study and volunteer work in an emergency room. He passed the state exam with a high grade and received his first EMT certificate. "I worked hard," he says. "But it didn't seem like work."

John then joined the volunteer ambulance corps in Westport. He also went back to college, first to Pace University to pick up basic courses, then to the University of Maryland, Baltimore County, to major in emergency health services. Because he was accepted as a sophomore, he finished his course work and internships in three years.

By his senior year, John was training as a cardiac rescue technician (CRT) with the Washington, D.C. Ambulance Service. Paramedics call it the "knife and gun club" because of the large number of stabbing and gun wounds they treat. Later he also trained at Children's Hospital in Washington, volunteered with a local fire department, and completed driving courses. Paramedics must learn to maneuver large ambulances through traffic and to deal with drivers who don't give up the right-of-way.

After John graduated from college, he accepted his present job. Since most paramedics in the Baltimore County Fire Department are cross-trained in both emergency medicine and firefighting, he spent 12 weeks training at the Fire Academy

Emergency Health Care

Emergency Medical Services (EMS) is designed to provide a 24-hour safety net of emergency health care for people throughout the United States. EMS is a complex system that varies from town to town, district to district, state to state. The service is activated when someone calls 911 or another emergency phone number.

The EMS system relies on both paid and volunteer workers. Paramedics traditionally work under local fire or police departments, but in some locations, they work in hospitals.

Some paramedics hold college degrees in emergency medicine, but many complete EMT training. The first level is a 100-hour course taught by police and fire departments, hospitals, and some colleges. To achieve the first level, registered EMT (Ambulance) trainees must complete the course and pass a written and practical exam. The second level is registered EMT (Intermediate). To become a registered EMT (Paramedic), you must have field experience before completing a three- to five-month training program. All registered EMTs pass written and practical tests. Registration requirements vary from state to state.

John Simone

before he was assigned to his paramedic position.

The Future

The field of emergency medicine is relatively new, but already it's changing. John predicts that future paramedics will be required to have more education, partly because of ever-changing technology.

As for his own future, John jokes that he will stay in emergency medicine until "it gets to be too much like a real job." The truth is he hasn't decided about his future. Because of the way the Baltimore County emergency system works, he may also choose to go into firefighting. Some paramedics decide to enter

other health fields, such as nursing, medicine, or physical therapy.

John recommends that anyone interested in emergency medicine begin training early. Informational programs about EMTs and firefighting are available for juniors and seniors in some high schools, and EMTs often speak to classes. Like many paramedics, John makes school presentations during Fire Safety Week. Volunteer fire departments, he says, are great places to get involved.

John checks supplies aboard the ambulance.

Karin Tobin

Chapter Two

SUBSTANCE ABUSE COUNSELOR

very few weeks Karin Tobin takes a group of teens on a field trip to the Shock Trauma Center, the emergency treatment facility of the University of Maryland. "We see people in a lot of pain and bleeding with their guts all over," she says. Her purpose is show the young people what can happen in automobile accidents—many of which are caused by alcohol and drug use.

As the adolescent substance abuse counselor for suburban Baltimore County, Karin is a government employee. The adolescents she counsels are often in trouble with drugs and alcohol. Most of them are referred to her by probation officers, teachers, or social workers who counsel families in crisis. She works one-on-one with young people and their parents. "I'm able to relate to kids on their level," she says. "I use their language." But she won't tolerate rudeness or disrespect. "I am not trying to be their friend," she says.

Karin's job requires a high level of energy and commitment, patience, and an ability to laugh and keep things in perspective. "I'm here to help people, not to save people," she says.

Self-Confidence Hour-long individual counseling sessions form the core of Karin's workday, which starts at 9:00 A.M. and ends at 6:00 P.M. "I see students who are referred to me because they got in trouble with the police," she says. "I find out about their life, friends, schools, what drugs they took, and how they get along with Mom and Dad." She also spends a few minutes talking separately with the parents.

After each session, Karin writes an assessment of the case—a summary of the adolescent's history of substance abuse and her recommendations for counseling and education. "You need the self-confidence to make a decision and defend that decision," she says. "You have to be able to write in a clear and understandable way."

Most of the adolescents Karin sees are required to attend her weekly substance abuse education classes. "I teach them what it does to their bodies," she says, "and what addiction looks like." In addition to teaching, Karin leads small group sessions with adolescents—mostly boys—who may be experimenting with drugs and alcohol. The confidential groups are designed to help these teens "figure out if they have a problem," she says. They learn to share their

experiences with the group and get feedback from others.

Twice a month, Karin attends meetings with representatives from other Baltimore County government agencies, including foster care, juvenile services, and mental health. "If someone has a case in which they can't figure out what to do, they bring it to the table and everyone offers options and feedback and specialized services," she says.

Karin also spends a lot of time on the phone, often taking calls from parents. Their worries may cause them to be short-tempered or unreasonable. "Parents are very difficult," says Karin. "I keep in the back of my mind what is causing their anger and feelings. Then I remind them that the problem has taken years to develop. I can't resolve it tomorrow. I let them know what I am capable of and willing to do."

Karin takes phone calls from teachers, parents, social workers, and the police.

Paperwork for insurance companies and other government agencies also takes a lot of Karin's time. She must fill out forms and write reports. "The paperwork shuffle gets confusing and frustrating," she says.

With her hectic days, Karin admits she needs help pacing herself. Her secretary plans her schedule. She also tries to take an occasional vacation day when her job gets too stressful. "I go skiing," she says.

Internship

Karin grew up north of Baltimore. A high school psychology course captured her interest. "I learned about emotions and how they related to people's behaviors," she says. "I could see it in the real world." She enrolled in a clinical psychology program at Towson State University, north of Baltimore.

Karin's course work included several internships, including one in a drug abuse center. She spent two years working 10 to 15 hours a week counseling people who were addicted to heroin, cocaine, PCP, and marijuana. "I ultimately grew to like it," she says. The director of the center became her mentor, or teacher.

Another internship took Karin to an inner-city elementary school to lead a self-esteem group. She also took a paying job as a part-time mental health worker at Shepherd Pratt Hospital, assisting nurses. Six months later, she began working with adolescents who had family problems, depression, or trouble controlling anger. She taught crafts classes and escorted her patients on field trips to movies or to see fireworks on the Fourth of

July. It's a job she still does part time. "I get to know people there on a long-term basis," she says. "It's good for me to see changes in kids."

Think Before You Drink

After college graduation, Karin became a counselor for mentally ill adults who were living independently in special apartments. "I walked around on hourly visits to make sure they were where they should be," she recalls. "I would escort people to the hospital. Then I decided I wasn't a babysitter for adults."

Her first job with Baltimore County was in AIDS education and community outreach. She made presentations to schools, churches,

I'm here to help people, not to save people.

and community groups. She also wrote a newsletter and created AIDS prevention campaigns. A campaign called "Think Before You Drink" promoted awareness about AIDS prevention. "Part of the job was wonderful," Karin says. "It made me feel good and channeled my energy, but after a year my creative juices were running low."

When the position for the adolescent counselor opened up, she was offered the job. Her psychology major, drug education experience, and background working with adolescents at Shepherd Pratt made her the perfect candidate for the job.

Professional Image

Many substance abuse counselors have either a high school degree and on-the-job experience or an associate degree in drug counseling from a community college. Karin believes, however, that a bachelor's degree will be necessary for most jobs in the future. She recommends majoring in social work, psychology, or sociology.

"The field of substance abuse counseling is a baby," she notes. "The field's going through a shift to a more professional image." Although no licenses or certifications are currently required for drug abuse counselors, Karin expects they will be in the future.

Substance abuse counselors work for treatment centers, hospitals, community centers, halfway houses, schools, and—like Karin—for government agencies. Salaries depend on education, professional experience, and level of responsibility.

Karin's advice to people interested in substance abuse counseling is to get involved in peer counseling programs in high school. She also suggests taking psychology courses in high school and college and talking to people in the field.

As for her own future, Karin says she loves her job, "but I have a lot of different ideas." They range from medical school to studying for a doctorate in psychology in order to teach at the college level or write books. So far, she's decided on just one thing: "I'm staying with adolescents. They are willing to try new things. And I enjoy their enthusiasm."

A *halfway house* is a residence for people who were formerly institutionalized in a hospital, prison, or drug treatment center. People who live in halfway houses get help readjusting to private life or living on their own.

License to Practice

Of the 12 health care professionals profiled in this book, only 2—the substance abuse counselor and the information systems manager—are not required to be licensed or certified or registered. Nurses, physical therapists, acupuncturists, nutritionists, dentists, paramedics, radiologic technologists, pharmacists, and psychologists must all meet certain standards of practice. Each state determines its own licensing requirements.

To be eligible for a license to practice in most health care fields, individuals must meet education requirements and pass written national tests or boards (and sometimes practical exams). In addition to knowledge of a particular field, these exams test knowledge of basic sciences such as biology, biochemistry, and anatomy. To be licensed, most health care providers must also complete internships or have work experience.

Professional associations set the standards for testing and usually give the exams. Licensing is a government function and varies from state to state.

To protect patients, the trend is toward tighter regulation of people working in the health care field. Jobs that do not involve treating patients—such as information systems manager—are less strictly regulated.

Steven Pohlhaus

Chapter Three

DENTIST

Sticking your hands in someone's mouth is pretty scary," says Dr. Steven Pohlhaus. "And the first time you feel like an idiot." Remembering his first patients in dental school, he jokes that they should be eligible for sainthood. "A little tiny filling takes you forever—three hours instead of ten minutes."

Dentistry is unique, Steve notes, because dentists often develop long-term relationships with patients. "You see kids grow up," he says. "Health care is too often very impersonal." His old-fashioned philosophy is evident in his relaxed, cheerful office. He even makes occasional house calls, using a mobile dental unit. "I can't do much," he says, "but it's often enough for patients who can't get out."

Intense Hours

Steve works with patients 32 hours a week. "They are intense hours, intellectually and physically demanding," he says. As a general practice dentist, he fills cavities, diagnoses and treats gum disease, takes impressions of people's mouths, and later fits crowns and bridgework, which replace broken or missing teeth.

Steven Pohlhaus

He also works with his patients to solve problems. For example, he might fit a special dental device for people who grind their teeth at night. "My practice is diverse," he explains. "I'm not doing one thing all day." Although he does some simple surgeries, he refers difficult cases to dental specialists such as oral surgeons. On average, Steve sees 10 to 15 patients a day.

His day typically begins at 8:00 A.M., with appointments scheduled until 1:00 P.M., when the office breaks for lunch. After lunch, appointments continue until 5:00 or 7:00 P.M. "Although I like to spend a little time with the patient, we try to stay on schedule," says Steve. "Waiting drives people nuts. We respect their time." But occasional emergencies—perhaps an infected or broken tooth—can

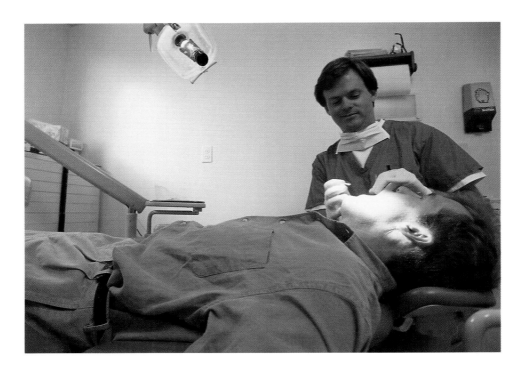

disrupt the day. "I'll see you whatever the problem is," he says. "This is not the field to be in if you can never stay late."

After the office closes, Steve attends to the work of running a small business, as most dentists must do. Using a computer, he pays taxes and bills and writes paychecks for his receptionists, dental assistants, and dental hygienist. He also writes and publishes an educational newsletter for his patients. The paperwork takes about four hours a week. "The only thing I don't like is dealing with the insurance stuff," he says. Like most health care providers, Steve must complete dozens of different forms for insurance companies in order to be paid. "It's frustrating, and it's not getting any better. It's getting worse."

Dental School

Steve majored in biology at Bucknell University in Pennsylvania. He became interested in dentistry after talking with friends who were already in dental school. After doing well on the Dental Admission Test (DAT), he was accepted into the four-year program at the University of Maryland's Dental School. He paid his way with scholarships, loans, and savings.

"The program is similar to medical school," he says. "The academic load is extremely high, with tons of reading. You're in class all day, watching lectures, or in the lab, working with the cadaver (corpse)." Dental students later learn how to do various procedures. They work first on models with plastic teeth and then on each other.

Steve's clinical, or practical, training began the summer between his sophomore and junior years. Under close supervision, he planned a course of treatment for each of the patients assigned to him at the dental school's low-cost community clinic. "You do everything on them," he says. Each student rotates to various clinics, such as oral surgery, emergency dentistry, and pediatric dentistry. Although Steve enjoyed the work, there was stress. "You have to do so many

You must inspire trust.

fillings and so many crowns. You are cramming a lot in." The American Dental Association may soon require one year of residency or additional training.

To be qualified to practice dentistry, Steve had to pass three sets of tests given by the American Dental Association. He took the first test, in basic sciences, during his second year of dental school. During his senior year, he passed another exam, testing his knowledge of dentistry and medicine. The third set of tests was clinical and written. He performed a dental procedure before a representative from the Northeast Regional Board. Each state has its own exam requirements. Steve is licensed to practice in Maryland.

After graduation, Steve did a general practice residency in a Veterans Administration Hospital, treating patients who had dental problems. Next he took a job with an established dentist. Being an associate dentist is often a necessary career step. "You have a boatload of debt, you're not that experienced, and your speed is not all that great," he says. "It's a good way to earn a predictable income." After a couple of years, he was itching to work for himself. "I was ready to deal with running a business," he says.

He applied for a low-interest loan and bought the practice he now owns from another dentist. "You buy equipment and goodwill," he says. "Although you're not buying patients, people have come here for years."

In addition to his practice, Steve teaches one day a week in an oral medicine clinic at the University of Maryland Dental School. "I love it," he says. He's also about to embark on his fourth trip with the Dominican Republic Dental Mission Project. For one month, a group of dentists and dental students bring modern equipment and techniques to rural areas in the Dominican Republic where there are no dentists. "Word gets around that the dentists will be there," he says. The American dentists also train Dominican dentists. This time, Steve will lead a small group deep into the mountains of the Dominican Republic for two weeks.

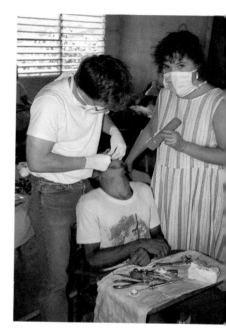

Steve does volunteer work in the Dominican Republic. Although the working conditions can be difficult, he is glad for the chance to help.

An Exciting Future

Steve believes the years ahead look bright for a dental career. "The field is more challenging," says Steve. "We don't just drill, fill, and bill. In one day I might do a filling, a root canal, a biopsy, and some surgery." About half of all dentists

Steven Pohlhaus

In the Dominican Republic, patients line up to receive dental treatment from Steve and other American dentists.

A *root canal* is a treatment to save a diseased tooth. A *biopsy* is surgery to remove a tissue sample. *Implants* are artificial teeth that can be surgically placed into the gums.

perform simple surgeries in their offices.

Technology is also being used more in dentistry. "The future is exciting," Steve says. "Implants, for example, can put teeth where you lost them."

But some things won't change. Dentists will always need to work with their hands and to communicate with their patients. "You stick sharp stuff in people's bodies," Steve says. "People are very vulnerable and scared. You must inspire trust."

Other Dental Careers

Dental assistants work alongside dentists, assisting the dentist with the instruments and mixing compounds for fillings. Some assistants perform clerical duties, such as scheduling patients and taking payments. Training is often on the job after high school graduation, although some college and vocational school programs award certificates or associate degrees. *Dental hygienists,* who are not directly supervised, are licensed professionals. The tasks they can perform are determined by each state. All hygienists clean teeth, take X rays, and teach patients proper brushing and flossing techniques. Dental hygienists have either a bachelor's or an associate degree from an accredited school of dental hygiene.

Dental laboratory technicians make and repair dentures, crowns (which cap broken or missing teeth), and other devices. Using wax impressions of the patient's mouth and following the dentist's instructions, they must work precisely. Although on-the-job training after high school is enough, many technicians enroll in technical schools for formal training and experience.

Steve's advice for future dentists is to "try to do well in school, but have a life. Learn how to deal with people. It's a big part of the job. And volunteer. It doesn't have to be in a health care place. Take extra time to do something with people."

Carolyn Hildreth

Chapter Four

PHYSICIAN

r. Carolyn Hildreth grew up in Chicago watching doctor shows on television. She never suspected that she would one day complete her own medical training at Cook County Hospital. It's the hospital that the television show "ER" is modeled on.

Dr. Hildreth—who prefers to be addressed by her professional title—is an internist, a general practitioner who treats adults. Now practicing in Baltimore, she stresses the importance of a healthy lifestyle. "Patients have to accept responsibility," she says. "In the 21st century, the emphasis will be on wellness."

Day and Night

Dr. Hildreth works long days. A typical weekday begins at 7:30 A.M. in the hospital, where she makes bedside visits to patients she has admitted. As an attending physician, she does exams, reviews test results, and writes instructions for the hospital staff.

Carolyn Hildreth

By 9:00 A.M., Dr. Hildreth is at her private office outside the hospital, seeing patients until 1:00 P.M. "Things tend to run over," she says. "I never get a break for any lunch." That's because she often takes extra time to encourage her patients to adopt a healthier lifestyle. "I discuss food preparation, go over a balanced diet, and recommend exercise three or four times a week."

It's hard for her to watch adults setting a bad example for their kids by smoking, keeping loaded guns around the house, and not wearing seat belts.

"Health doesn't end at the doctor's door," she says. "In many cases, I take care of an entire family, two or three generations. This is what makes each day something to look forward to."

One afternoon a week, she rushes to Baltimore City Community College, where she's the staff physician. On other days, she sees patients in her office until 5:00 or 6:00 P.M., or attends continuing education lectures, called Grand Rounds, at a local hospital.

And then there are the emergencies. "I am on call 7 days a week, 24 hours a day," says Dr. Hildreth. Like most doctors, she isn't crazy about being called for nonemergencies in the middle of the night. During real emergencies, she coordinates hospital and emergency care. "I don't have to go to the ER," she says. Instead, she stays in touch with emergency room doctors and cares for the patient after admission to the hospital.

Dr. Hildreth spends Saturdays dealing with the hurricane of paperwork that accompanies medicine: billing, ordering supplies, preparing taxes, and submitting insurance forms. She doesn't let it get her down. "I have a good accountant and a good banker," she says. "I just deal with it."

Medical School

After graduating as valedictorian from her high school in Chicago, Dr. Hildreth studied biology at Vassar College in New York state. She already had volunteer experience in a community hospital, first in the emergency room, then as an EKG (electrocardiogram) technician. She volunteered at a local hospital during college, working as an EKG technician on Saturdays.

During her last year at Vassar, Dr. Hildreth took the Medical College Admission Test (MCAT), then applied to 10 medical schools. She was accepted at four schools in her hometown, Chicago. She chose the University of Illinois.

"Health doesn't end at the doctor's door.

"Medical school is quite a bit of fun," she says. "It's challenging. It's a process. You look toward the end and meet the challenge." She also acknowledges that it can be stressful, with two or three times as much work as in college. The first year, after classes and labs all day, she studied late into the night.

The second year brought a combination of classes and clinical experience. "You begin to learn how to interview patients and conduct a physical exam," says Dr. Hildreth. She also

Medical Specialties versus Family Practice

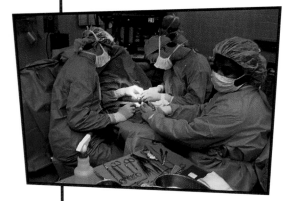

At present, the United States has two specialists for every family doctor. Experts believe it should be the other way around, because they think that the need for specialists will decrease. In the coming years, more young doctors may be encouraged to train as internists or as family practioners (doctors who treat both adults and children).

Physicians who become specialists— surgeons, cardiologists, psychiatrists, ear, nose, and throat doctors, and others— may complete longer residencies after medical school than family practitioners and internists. Their salaries are often higher. Medical specialists also tend to be more oriented toward new procedures and high technology.

Most future doctors will work for someone else— not for themselves in a private practice. Many will be employed by large practices that hire many physicians and an administrative staff to handle paperwork. Other employers will be health maintenance organizations (HMOs), hospitals, or health clinics run by nonprofit or government organizations. And all physicians have to keep up with the latest technologies.

began to learn about various diseases and their signs and symptoms.

She spent the entire third and fourth years of medical school doing clinical rotations in various branches of medicine. Dr. Hildreth spent 12 weeks each in internal medicine and general surgery and 8 weeks each in pediatrics (working with children) and OB/GYN (obstetrics and gynecology—the branches of medicine that deal with women's health and reproduction). Her electives, or nonrequired courses, were psychiatry (mental health), orthopedics (bones and joints), ophthalmology (eyes), and ENT (ear, nose, and throat).

The hours were long, and often Dr. Hildreth was at the hospital seven days a week. "I never found I was so tired I was past making good judgments," she says. "I wanted

Dr. Hildreth checks a patient's blood pressure. She encourages her patients to adopt healthier lifestyles.

to be there. Patients saw me more than attending physicians. You feel some commitment to them, and you should."

As for the often shocking side of medicine, she says, "I wasn't a bit squeamish with blood. I was fine with it."

Internship and Residency

After finishing medical school and passing her state boards, Dr. Hildreth continued her training for four more years, beginning with a year of paid internship. Interns are physicians, but they are not licensed to practice. They gain practical experience under the supervision of residents and attending physicians. After internship comes residency. (Internship is actually the first year of residency.) The number of years of residency varies, depending on the specialty. Residents broaden their knowledge and supervise interns and medical students.

Dr. Hildreth worked for two more years as a resident in internal medicine at Cook County Hospital in Chicago. It's an inner-city facility, where patients are often the poorest of the poor. "I loved my patients," she says, but she still shakes with anger and disgust when she remembers the conditions: cockroaches, not enough supplies, and outdated equipment.

She worked 8 to 10 hours a day and was on call from 8:00 P.M. to 8:00 A.M. every fourth night. "If danger arose, we could deal with it," says Dr. Hildreth. "It's not really a question of what to do. You learn what to do. Things become usual."

Boards refers to a test or tests given by an examining board, which is usually part of a professional association.

Dr. Hildreth's medical school education was paid for by the Health Services Corps, a federal government program. In return, she agreed to work for four years in a public health care institution. Her first job was in a public health clinic. Although the neighborhood was desperately poor, she enjoyed her patients. After three years, she left to spend two years at the University of Maryland Hospital, then finished her Health Services Corps commitment as a doctor for a federal prison in New York. "It was horrible," she says. "You get to see what prison is like."

Dr. Hildreth returned to Baltimore to practice. After one year at a local hospital, she opened a private practice. In addition to building her practice, Dr. Hildreth plans to continue to bring her message of wellness to local residents, particularly those in the inner city. She participates in conferences and health fairs in the community.

"If you want to go into medicine," Dr. Hildreth says, "you don't have to be a genius. You need to be a well-rounded person." You also don't have to study just science and math in college. "You have plenty of time to learn biochemistry," she says. "Get a feel for hospital work and working with doctors." She suggests following a doctor for a day if you can. "You need to work with people and know you will be comfortable. Work in a nursing home or homeless shelter," she says.

Evan Rosenberg

Chapter Five

MEDICAL INFORMATION SYSTEMS MANAGER

The hospital of the future will seem like science fiction, says medical information systems manager Evan Rosenberg. Hospital beds outfitted with computers will take a patient's weight and blood pressure. Nurses will log patient information in notebook computers. Doctors will review X rays, order tests, and admit new patients from their homes or offices—or anywhere in the world. Computers that understand human speech will respond to patients. And, perhaps as a reminder that a living, breathing person is still there, a picture of the patient will appear on the computer monitor for a doctor checking on a patient from a distant office.

In about eight years, Evan helped bring Baltimore's Sinai Hospital very close to this futuristic vision. "When I came," he says, "to do an X ray, a doctor had to fill out forms and send them through interoffice mail." Now the computer orders the test and a patient's transportation to the X ray department, then sends the results to the doctor and bills the insurance company. The number of computer terminals has catapulted from 35 to 500. "Computers save money, improve patient care, and help things run more smoothly," says Evan.

24 Hours a Day

Evan begins his day around 8:00 A.M. by listening to his voice mail and logging onto the computer to read and respond to his e-mail. Most of it comes from hospital supervisors. "I very rarely write to someone on paper," he says. As a project manager, he is free to set his own schedule.

Meetings consume a lot of his time. "I meet with managers of departments who have ideas about how the computer can help them," he says. For example, the radiology department wanted doctors who were not on Sinai's staff to be able to receive a patient's test results. "We redesigned the software to make it do that," says Evan. "I figure out what the computer needs to do to solve their problem: what screens need to come up, what kinds of information people need to put in, how the computer should store information, and what commands need to be typed in to execute the program."

**Evan oversees a large
network of computers
at Sinai Hospital.**

The next step is to modify the software by writing or rewriting the millions of lines of internal code that tell the software program how to work. "I go from a language we understand to a language the computer understands," he says. Most of the programming is done by the four programmers Evan supervises. "I end up doing less programming and more and more designing what the system should do," he says.

Later, the program is run, then debugged. "If we take the computer system from the user," he says, "we must find time when they're not using it." That's often in the middle of the night.

Evan eats lunch at his desk, often signing on to the Internet through his personal account. He spends his afternoon in meetings and planning future computer systems. He estimates that a third of his time is spent on new projects, overseeing the construction

Evan Rosenberg

and wiring of fiber optic networks, managing the budget, and purchasing equipment.

Another part of Evan's job is training. He teaches the trainers, who in turn teach hospital employees how to use the computer systems. "Technology is hard for people to understand. You have to tolerate people's lack of understanding of what technology is and how it can help," he says.

Although Evan's day ends around 6:00 P.M., he is on call around the clock. Once he even carried a satellite beeper with him on a vacation to Mexico. That's unusual, but he knows he can often solve problems long distance during a crisis. "When the computer goes down, people first say, 'We survived for 100 years without it.' Then the phone begins to ring," he says. "We go weeks without calls. Other times, it's really bad."

A Psychology Major

Evan's career path has been anything but direct. He graduated from the University of Maryland with a degree in psychology. His first two jobs were in psychiatric hospitals, assisting psychologists with patients who needed help with living skills. Evan soon realized that he needed a doctorate in psychology to advance in his career. Since that would mean years of graduate study, he decided against it. Instead he took a job managing a stereo store, then enrolled part time in a technical school to learn computer programming.

"I did very well in school," Evan says. But his job search wasn't so easy. "I sent out 350 resumes. I was as low as I could have gotten."

Finally he landed a job with a software developer. He worked on a project-by-project basis, mostly for small telephone companies that needed computer software after the breakup of the huge telecommunications company AT&T. Evan later worked for Toyota for two years, writing programs to help managers keep track of auto parts. Then he took a position with a consulting firm. When someone contacted him about a job at Sinai Hospital, he was ready to move on.

During his eight years at Sinai, Evan also finished a master's degree in information technology at Johns Hopkins University. The program was oriented more toward management than computer programming, he says.

"I'm surprised I'm still doing programming," says Evan. "There's usually a lot of repetition. But at Sinai it's constantly changing." He believes good programers need to be analytical, patient, and more detail minded than people oriented. "I have to tolerate a high amount of frustration," he says. "Sometimes programs don't work." What Evan likes best about working with computers is the creativity. "You are solving problems," he says, "finding unique solutions all the time."

Exploding Technology

Evan notes that computer technology in the medical field is exploding. He believes that as medical software becomes more user-friendly, there will be much less need for programmers. "Knowledge of the medical side will be more important than the computer side," he says. It's hard for him

Evan Rosenberg

to predict what kind of education will be most useful. "Try community colleges," he suggests. "They are responding more quickly and are more technology oriented."

As for Evan's own future, he recently accepted a new position as director of

> # I have to tolerate a high amount of frustration. Sometimes programs don't work.

information systems for Johns Hopkins Home Care Group. He will set up state-of-the-art computer systems for home health care nurses.

For those interested in a career in medical information systems, Evan recommends doing volunteer work and summer internships in a hospital to get comfortable with the medical language and environment. Extensive computer experience in and out of school is very valuable. He also recommends computer camps.

Volunteer Work

Most hospitals and nursing homes welcome volunteers. Larger institutions have volunteer coordinators who conduct formal orientation programs and place volunteers in departments that need help. Tasks may include transporting patients on stretchers and in wheelchairs. Some volunteers read to patients or take care of flowers and gifts. Older students who are interested in health care professions are often trained for specific jobs, such as EKG technicians and nurse's aides.

Most hospitals and nursing homes require student volunteers to be at least 16 years old. In nursing homes, younger students may accompany parents or participate in a Pets-on-Wheels type of program to bring family animals to cheer bedridden patients.

Magaly Rodriguez de Bittner

Chapter Six

PHARMACIST

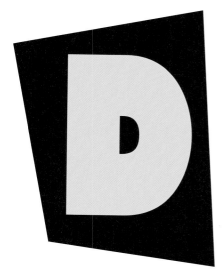

r. Magaly Rodriguez de Bittner will be the first to tell you her job doesn't resemble that of the community pharmacist most people know. She is Assistant Professor of Pharmacy at the University of Maryland. Instead of filling prescriptions, she is helping define a new role for pharmacists in the 21st century.

Pharmacists of the future, Magaly says, will take a more active role in patient care: they will become health educators. "If I give you a cholesterol drug, why can't I teach you about diet?" she asks. She predicts a time when patients will see a pharmacist the way they now visit the doctor. Patients may even go to a pharmacy for some medical tests.

And who will fill prescriptions? Probably computerized robots in large mail-order companies. Computers can already fill 10,000 prescriptions a day with great accuracy, compared to 200 for an average pharmacist. With competition like that, Magaly says, "pharmacists will have to prove themselves in the community or disappear. It's an exciting and dangerous time for pharmacists."

Each Day Is Different

Magaly's schedule varies from semester to semester. Teaching, research, and committee work form a triangle of responsibilities. Although she works Monday through Friday, few days are the same. "I get in at 7:00 A.M. or 8:00 A.M. or 9:00 A.M.: whenever I have to be here," she says. She must juggle an often overwhelming schedule. Little or no clerical help is a big frustration.

As a teacher, Magaly chooses textbooks for courses, prepares and gives lectures, grades exams, and is available to her students at certain hours. She also serves on several faculty committees, including the admissions committee, which interviews all prospective pharmacy students. Meetings take up a big chunk of her time.

Then there's her research. Depending on the number of courses she is teaching—which can vary from none to three—Magaly makes time to plan and conduct research. To study a drug, she begins by developing a protocol—a standard for the drug's use, including the dosage and how the drug should be taken. Her next step is to study patients who use the drug, documenting the results of the drug therapy. The goal is to determine how a drug works best. Her final step is to write and publish articles about her findings. Two or three times a year, she may also attend conferences to present research papers to other pharmacists and physicians.

Magaly's job is a shared position. In addition to teaching at the University of Maryland School of Pharmacy, Magaly also has patients at the Veterans Administration Hospital. She spends one afternoon a week in the Medicine Refill Clinic at the hospital. "Instead of seeing an M.D., patients come and see me," she says. She interviews patients, asking questions about their medications and when they last saw a doctor. Then she collects data such as blood pressure and pulse rate. "We are responsible for reviewing a patient's medicine, making sure there are no drug interactions or problems with the medications," she says. She may also consult a physician for a second opinion or send a very sick patient to the emergency room.

Magaly's patients have diseases such as diabetes or liver disease and must take medication at all times. They have all been seen previously by a doctor. In the state of Maryland, she says, pharmacists cannot

Magaly discusses a prescription with a patient at the Veterans Hospital.

refill certain prescriptions without a doctor's orders. In a few states, pharmacists have limited prescribing privileges.

Magaly's academic and hospital days end when the job is done. "Because you are providing a service, you don't just leave at six," she says. "And you must be available through your beeper."

Pharmacy School

When Magaly was growing up in Puerto Rico, she wanted to be a doctor. But she was put off by the long training. Instead she enrolled in a five-year pharmacy program at the University of Puerto Rico. The program included two years of science and math courses, followed by three years of professional pharmacy studies. As part of their school program, pharmacy students also complete a four- to six-month supervised internship in a community or hospital pharmacy. Many students also work as pharmacy technicians— at the front counter helping the pharmacist refill prescriptions.

After graduation, Magaly took the national written exam so she could get her license. The exam tested her knowledge of drugs, their side effects, and the possible problems of taking more than one drug at a time. For the most part, licensing requirements are the same throughout the United States. Two states, however (including Maryland), require students to pass a practical test. It involves making up different kinds of prescriptions.

After college, Magaly worked for a year and a half in a community pharmacy in Puerto Rico. "But I couldn't see myself

behind the counter forever," she says. Choosing the University of Maryland, she spent two years getting her doctorate in pharmacy, which included a residency at the Veterans Administration hospital. "The level of practice is more sophisticated at the doctoral level," she says. "It's similar to an M.D., more practical and hands-on. We also do a lot of lectures for nurses and doctors about different new drugs."

Hospital Pharmacist

After getting her Pharm. D. degree, Magaly worked for five years as a clinical hospital pharmacist at the VA Hospital. She monitored patients' drugs and made rounds visiting patients as part of a medical team with the doctors and

" It's an exciting and dangerous time for pharmacists. "

nurses. The teamwork occasionally caused friction. "Doctors are not used to others invading their territory," she says. "But they need to recognize that as science evolves, things get more complex. M.D.'s don't have the time or training to become experts in drugs. Pharmacists are experts."

She enjoyed her years as a full-time clinical pharmacist. "What I like best is having the opportunity to make a difference

Community and Hospital Pharmacists

The vast majority of pharmacists work in community pharmacies. They fill prescriptions, order drugs, monitor the storage of drugs, oversee the pharmacy technicians who work the front counters, and provide information to patients. Community pharmacists must follow insurance regulations and laws. Many pharmacists work for large chain stores. Much of the day is spent in front of a computer, entering patient information and checking for drug interactions or incorrect dosages.

Pharmacists also talk to physicians by phone to check any special instructions. Although pharmacists can and do occasionally make up special compounds or ointments, most drugs come ready for them to count out. Experienced pharmacists manage the prescription department and earn larger salaries. Many large pharmacies are open during the evening and on weekends.

Hospital pharmacists have a somewhat different role. Most rarely see a patient, but, like community pharmacists, they follow the physician's orders and supervise technicians. Hospital pharmacists make up medication carts or drawers for each patient, first making sure there are no drug interactions or dosage errors. Since hospitals are increasingly computerized, hospital pharmacists also spend a large part of the day entering patient and drug information into the computer. Hospital pharmacists must be available around the clock, so they may work some night shifts.

in people's lives, to help others," she says. But she's once again looking to the future. As part of her research at the University of Maryland, she is working with a large chain of drugstores to develop and open a pharmaceutical care center near Baltimore. It will be a pharmacy for the future, one of the first in the country in which the pharmacist provides direct patient care.

Magaly offers some advice if you are thinking about a career in pharmacy. "Go and observe a pharmacist to get a feeling for what it's all about," she says. "Deliver prescriptions for the day." She also suggests volunteering in a nursing home or hospital to see if you like working with people. Another idea is to find a summer job, volunteer or paid, working with a pharmacist in a clinic or lab. Her last suggestion? Study science.

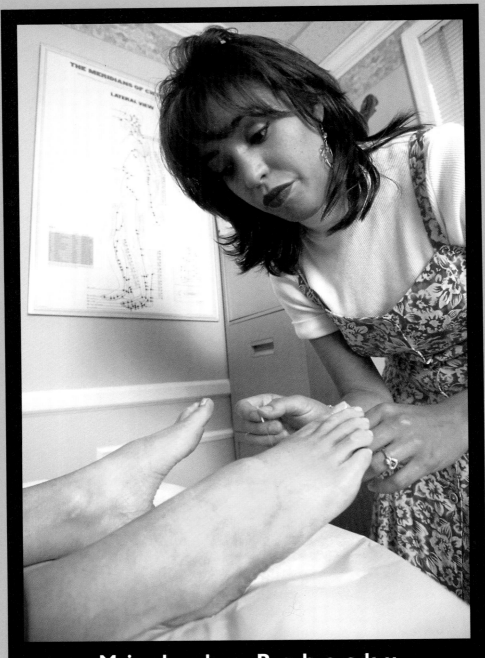

Michele Rohosky

Chapter Seven

ACUPUNCTURIST

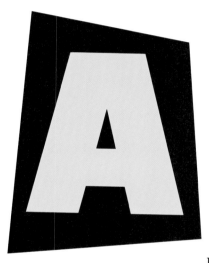

cupuncturist Michele Rohosky treats her patients with an ancient system of healing that is mysterious to most Westerners. By inserting slender needles into various parts of a patient's body, she can often relieve pain and treat diseases more effectively than many more modern medical methods. Acupuncture, she says, is based on "creating harmony with the body, mind, spirit, and nature." Treatments can clear sinuses, ease depression and anxiety, help insomnia, and relieve back and headache pain.

Sometimes acupuncture is used along with modern medical treatments to reduce pain or to stabilize the body after surgery. "Acupuncture doesn't work for anything that needs fixing now," Michele says, "like broken bones and bleeding wounds."

Although acupuncture has been used successfully for over 3,000 years—mostly in China, Korea, and Japan—how it works remains something of a mystery. Acupuncturists believe that the slender needles release the flow of energy in the body and help restore balance, or health.

These ideas may seem unscientific or bizarre to people in Western cultures. And although acupuncture is increasingly popular with patients and some doctors, others remain skeptical of its benefits. There are even a few states where acupuncture is not legal, despite long training and high standards of cleanliness for all acupuncturists. But, Michele says, "The door is opening."

An Acupuncture Session

Michele is completing the final semester of a two-and-a-half year program at the Traditional Acupuncture Institute in Maryland. As part of her program, she sees patients from 9:00 A.M. to 5:00 P.M. three days a week at the school, giving 10 to 15 treatments each day.

In a typical acupuncture treatment, Michele first talks at length with her patient. She notices the sound of the patient's voice, the color of the face and tongue, and any odors and obvious emotions. Then she takes the patient's pulse.

Acupuncturists feel for six pulse positions on each wrist—three on the surface and three deep down. The pulses help Michele decide which treatment to perform. "We never do exactly the same treatment," she says.

Michele then inserts sterile needles no thicker than a human hair into any of 365 points along 12 meridians, or vertical channels, in the body. Acupuncturists believe that energy flows along these vertical lines. The channels cannot be seen, although

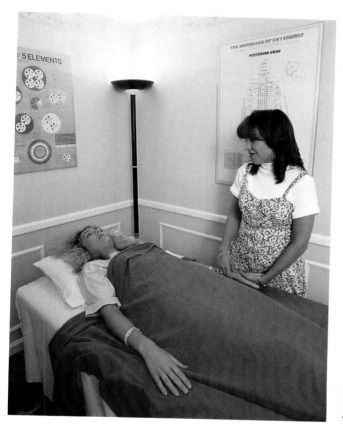

Michele talks with a patient before giving her an acupuncture treatment.

patients sometimes feel slight electrical impulses along them.

During an acupuncture treatment, there is no blood and little pain. Usually the needles are left in for a period of time. Michele finishes the treatment by removing the needles and taking the patient's pulses again to determine if there has been a change.

Treatments take between 30 minutes and an hour, although the first time she sees someone, Michele may spend up to two hours. Most acupuncture patients need a series of treatments to get relief from their symptoms. Like all health care providers,

Michele Rohosky

Michele keeps written records of treatments and files insurance claims for patients. "Paperwork is the worst," she says.

A Family Profession

Both Michele's mother and stepfather are acupuncturists, but during college she never considered an acupuncture career. "No way," she laughs, "too flaky." Instead, when she graduated from the University of Maryland, she planned to become a psychologist. "But I found something was missing," she says. "I didn't feel like it was incorporating all levels I feel in myself."

Then she had a car accident. "Doctors told me I'd have arthritis in my foot and I wouldn't play sports," she recalls. I was in a cast for three months." Her first acupuncture treatment left her free of pain. She was hooked.

She applied to the Traditional Acupuncture Institute and spent a year taking the required courses in nutrition, anatomy (the study of the parts of the body), and physiology (the processes of the body). She also volunteered at a local hospital. To learn firsthand about the human body, the students also trained in massage therapy or other bodywork. Michele studied evenings at the Baltimore School of Massage.

Although there are different kinds of acupuncture, the most common is called the Five Elements. (This is the method taught at the Traditional Acupuncture Institute.) The use of the five elements for healing—fire, earth, metal, water, and wood—does not correspond to anything in Western medicine.

During the first full-time year, students at the Traditional Acupuncture Institute learn interviewing skills, acupuncture theory, techniques for diagnosing various health problems, and the location of the many meridian points used in treatments. Many acupuncturists also study the use of Chinese herbs.

"Needles aren't used for the first year," Michele says. "It's all theory, and finding points, touching them with your finger, and finding out what a point feels like." At first students learn to use needles in oranges and pincushions, Michele says. Later, they practice on themselves and each other. "It's very difficult," she says. "You learn by doing."

After a needle ceremony—when students are presented with their first needle—they continue to learn by observing their teachers give treatments. Later students give actual treatments under supervision.

To graduate, Michele must complete 125 separate treatments and observe another 125 treatments by other students. She also must complete her senior project, writing what she calls a "spirit notebook" in which she describes in detail each of the 365 acupuncture points. After graduation, she will apply for her acupuncture license from the state.

"Acupuncture is such a pure therapy," she says. "What I like so much about it is that it's not limited. There's always something I don't know. And when you are one with yourself, things will flow. Something that was hard before may be easy. The more you learn about yourself, the more you can help others."

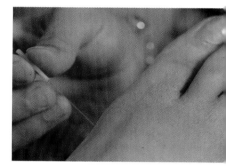

The needles used in acupuncture are extremely thin— thinner than a human hair.

Michele Rohosky

A Bright Future

"Acupuncture is exploding," says Michele. More and more doctors refer their patients to acupuncturists for conditions such as back pain and headaches. Some insurance companies pay for acupuncture. Government researchers are studying how and why acupuncture works. Even racehorses and athletes get treatments to improve their performance and health.

> # The more you learn about yourself, the more you can help others.

Most acupuncturists are self-employed. They charge for their work by the hour. Upon graduation, Michele plans to work in her stepfather's practice before opening her own office. "In school they don't teach you about how to set up an office," she says. "In the future, I may teach or maybe do a book."

Reading books is one way to learn about acupuncture. And since it's important for an acupuncturist to want to help others, Michele suggests volunteer work in a hospital or nursing home. It might also be possible to find an acupuncturist who would be willing to talk to your class. The very best way to learn about acupuncture? "Get a treatment."

Chiropractic Care

Chiropractors believe that many illnesses are caused by a disturbance of the body's nervous system, the internal communication system made up of brain, nerves, and spinal cord. They treat patients by manipulating the spinal column, which holds bundles of nerves. This treatment is meant to ease blockages of nerve impulses to other parts of the body. Chiropractors talk to patients and observe them, then do physical examinations to learn which parts of the skeleton are misaligned, or out of place. Like acupuncturists, chiropractors do not use drugs or surgery. Unlike acupuncturists, they do use laboratory tests—such as blood tests—and X rays to diagnose problems.

Chiropractors in all states must be licensed to practice. Many complete an associate or bachelor's degree in science before they apply to a four-year chiropractic college. After graduation, they take state boards or written examinations.

Most chiropractors work in private practices, either alone or with other chiropractors. Salaries can be high after a few years, although like all self-employed health professionals, they must provide their own health and vacation benefits.

Dirk Le Flore

Chapter Eight

REGISTERED NURSE

urse Dirk Le Flore knows all too well about pain and suffering. A home health care nurse, Dirk treats people with AIDS who are in the later stages of the disease. He sees firsthand how devastating the disease can be for individuals and families. "I'm not only working with the patient, but the whole family," he says. "You need to be sympathetic, caring, patient, knowledgeable, and goal oriented."

Dirk understands that AIDS affects caregivers, too. Although he knows how the virus spreads and uses a mask and gloves, he remembers the anxiety he felt when he saw his first AIDS patient. "I walked into his room and stood there," he says. "I couldn't move. I wouldn't sit down or touch anything." The next day, he confided his irrational fears to his patient . "He said, 'I understand,'" Dirk recalls. Dirk's fears were eased, and the barrier between them broke down.

Dirk Le Flore

Home Health Care

As a home health care nurse, Dirk treats a wide range of patients, from people who are totally independent to people who are near death. He works Monday through Friday starting at about 7:00 A.M. and sees eight or more patients each day. He uses a car phone and a beeper to stay in touch with his patients and the home health care service that employs him.

During a home visit, Dirk assesses his patient's condition and asks about diet. He may draw blood and administer drugs through an IV (a tube used to give fluids intravenously, that is, through the veins). He also educates his patients about their

Dirk starts an IV for a patient with AIDS.

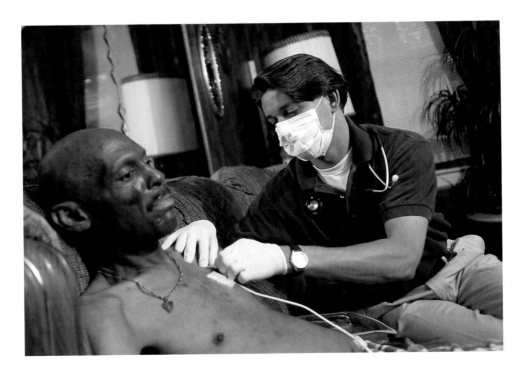

medicines and what to do in an emergency. Finally, since his patients are sometimes on experimental drugs, he watches for unusual symptoms. "I'm the physician's eyes and ears," he says. He spends a quarter to half of his time keeping records on his patients.

But Dirk's job involves more than the medical side. He is often the main support for family members and patients, helping them

I'm the physician's eyes and ears.

deal with the emotional aspects of having a fatal disease. As an AIDS patient nears death, Dirk may discuss funeral arrangements and arrange grief counseling.

In addition to his home health care work, Dirk oversees a local health clinic one night a week. "It's a break from home care," he says. "I like the camaraderie."

A Family of Nurses

Dirk grew up in a small Oklahoma town where his father was an agricultural teacher and the town's unofficial veterinarian. He often went with his dad to treat sick animals. And both Dirk and his sister—also a nurse now—visited with the residents of a nursing home where his mother worked as a nurse.

After taking math and science courses in high school, Dirk attended Northeastern State University in Oklahoma. After two years, he transferred to the University of Oklahoma in Norman. After two and a half more years, he completed the clinical (practical) part of his bachelor's degree at the Health Sciences Center in Oklahoma City.

Like medical students, nursing students learn on the job. At first Dirk spent one morning a week in the hospital, giving bed baths and handling other personal chores. Patient care wasn't new for him. To pay for school, he had worked in two hospitals, first transporting patients and later as a certified nursing assistant on a cancer unit.

By their senior year, student nurses can start IVs, draw blood, and administer drugs under supervision. Dirk became comfortable working with AIDS patients, IV drug users, and cancer patients, but he found it hard to treat children. "I just knew in my heart I couldn't work with them," he recalls. "It's too traumatic."

After graduation, Dirk took the written national boards (exams) to become a registered nurse (RN). He failed the first time but passed it six months later. Licensing is handled by individual states. Dirk is licensed to practice in Louisiana, Oklahoma, Texas, New York, and Maryland.

Traveling Nurse

After graduation, Dirk took a job as a night staff nurse. His responsibilities included "a head-to-toe assessment" of each patient: taking vital signs (pulse, breathing, blood pressure, and temperature), listening to lungs, checking to make sure IVs weren't

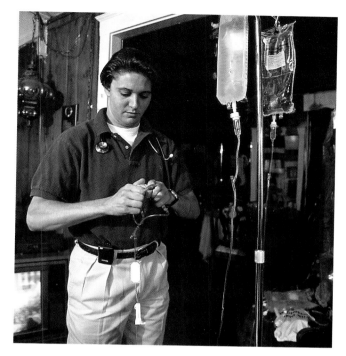

Home health care nurses face a variety of challenges each day.

clogged, changing surgical dressings, and giving medications.

Many of his patients were undergoing chemotherapy, a painful and frightening procedure used to treat cancer. "I would stay with them," he says. "The sicker the patients, the less down time. Most of the time you are on your feet, running."

After a year and a half, Dirk signed up with a company that placed nurses on short-term assignments in different parts of the country. He applied by phone and sent his license and resume.

His first job, at a state hospital in Lubbock, Texas, was a shocker. Assigned as "charge nurse," he was responsible for the entire nursing staff in the kidney transplant ward. "It was scary," he says. "I had no experience whatsoever." The assignment lasted eight weeks. "I learned to be flexible," he says.

Dirk's next assignment was at Johns Hopkins Hospital in Baltimore. He drove east, only to discover that the position promised him was not open. His company quickly assigned him to another local hospital. "But I hated it," he says. "There were a lot of gun wounds and car accidents. And I had 12 or 14 patients, so there was no way I could give good physical care." A newspaper ad for home health care nurses led him to his present job.

The Future of Nursing

The future for nurses is bright. With health care costs rising, nurses are taking on more responsibility. "We're going to see more specialty nursing," says Dirk. Emergency and critical care units already require that nurses have additional training.

Dirk plans to get a master's degree eventually. "I would love to teach, but I need more education," he says. For the near future, he is considering working full time in a clinic. "The death and dying is taking its toll," he says of his work with AIDS patients. "And I love the clinic setting. It's not as formal as a hospital." It also doesn't come with quite as much record keeping. "Paperwork takes me away from my patients," he says.

For students who want to enter nursing, Dirk suggests volunteering in a hospital or going to work for a day with a parent or neighbor who works at a hospital or clinic.

Nursing Careers

Nurse's aides, or certified nursing assistants, have the fewest responsibilities of the nursing staff. Most are trained on the job. *Licensed practical nurses* (LPNs) train full time for at least a year after high school, then pass a written test to become licensed. Community colleges, vocational schools, and hospitals all offer approved courses. In the future, LPNs will probably need at least two years of college and training.

Although many *registered nurses* (RNs) have a bachelor's degree in nursing, three-year hospital-based programs are also available. Graduates from these programs take the same national test to become RNs as college graduates do. Administrators and charge nurses, who are responsible for a unit, usually have at least a bachelor's degree.

Nurses work in hospitals, home health care services, corporations, HMOs, doctor's offices, rehabilitation centers, nursing homes, and schools. Salaries depend on education, experience, and location. Home health care nurses are paid well, but they must usually pay for their own health insurance.

Elisabeth Keep

Chapter Nine

NUTRITIONIST

ood is neither good nor bad," says nutritionist Elisabeth Keep. But she knows that food can have tremendous power. Some of her clients have eating disorders such as anorexia, a deadly disease of self-starvation. When food becomes the enemy, it can have destructive power. "Food issues and overeating are always related to feelings and emotions," she says.

Elisabeth is a part-time nutritionist at the Bennett Institute of Sports and Rehabilitative Medicine in Baltimore. As part of a team of health care specialists—along with an exercise technician and a nurse—she conducts classes and offers nutritional counseling for people who have had heart disease. She also counsels private patients. And she practices what she preaches. "If I didn't appear to be healthy, no one would take me seriously," she says.

Full Days

Arriving at her office at 7:30 A.M., Elisabeth answers her mail and reviews her schedule for the day. Individual counseling sessions—for her private clients and for those in the cardiac program—must be woven among the four hour-long classes she teaches.

Elisabeth Keep

These classes, part of a 12-week Cardiac Rehabilitation Program, help people make changes to reduce their chance of future heart disease.

"We monitor their weight," Elisabeth explains, "and teach about nutrition. In between classes, people see me for appointments to talk about how they are doing." The results can be gratifying. "I see people who make changes in their life nutritionally," she says. "I feel good about it."

On Thursdays, Elisabeth sees new cardiac patients. They may already have seen a psychologist and nurse, and Elisabeth reviews the files from those meetings. "I try to know a little about the person and get my educational materials together," she says. Then she does an assessment. She evaluates the kinds of food the person usually eats, analyzes the results of lab work (such as blood cholesterol tests), and tries to understand the patient's lifestyle.

What she doesn't do is hand out the same diet for everyone. Instead, she asks about what foods her patients like, when they eat, and how much time they have to prepare meals. Then she makes recommendations, which might include limiting meat, butter, or mayonnaise in their diet.

Elisabeth is also building her private practice. Her job arrangement with Bennett Institute allows her to use her office at the Institute to see additional patients. Many of these people, who are referred to her by doctors, have eating disorders.

"I am trying to bring them toward normal eating behavior," she says. "It's a very slow process."

In addition to anorexia, she also treats bulimia and compulsive overeating. Since eating disorders are often associated with other problems, such as childhood abuse, she works in a team with a psychologist or psychiatrist. "We work on ways to eat healthy and utilize stress reduction techniques," she says.

Elisabeth's counseling appointments and classes are scheduled tightly. In between, she makes phone calls, writes up her assessments, and does the billing for her private clients. Her day ends at 4:30 or 7:30 P.M., depending on the day.

Dealing with the money is the part of her work she likes least. "It's hard when someone needs your help and can't afford it," she says.

Elisabeth helps her clients develop healthy eating habits.

Most insurance companies will not pay for her services.

Health Science Project

Unlike many people, Elisabeth knew early on what she wanted to do for a living. "I've always been interested in food," she says. "My first job was in a bakery. I also worked in a Baskin-Robbins and a pizza parlor. And I was a Good Humor (ice cream) girl." A high school science project on vitamins and food additives further whetted her interest.

After high school, Elisabeth attended Rutgers University in New Jersey, majoring in human nutrition and food service management. Her courses included human anatomy and physiology, biochemistry, and organic chemistry. "You have to really like science," she says. Other courses included human nutrition, food service, diet therapy, and food testing.

Taking a job as a food service director in a nursing home, she planned meals and monitored portions. She also taught nutrition part time in a continuing education program. Next came a position with Grummon Aerospace on Long Island. Hired to start a corporate wellness program, Elisabeth counseled groups and individuals. She trained the chefs and created healthier menus. "I got the job because I had both food service and nutrition education experience," she says. Elisabeth believes that food service and nutritional counseling cannot be separated. "You have to know what the kitchen is capable of and be aware of the budget," she says.

When her job at Grummon was eliminated because of budget cutting, she took a position at a nearby hospital working with

> ## " You have to really like science. "

cardiac patients. During this time, she studied for a master's degree in medical biology at Long Island University. After graduation, Elisabeth passed the national written test given by the American Dietetic Association to become a registered nutritionist.

Three years ago, the part-time job at Bennett Institute opened, and she jumped at the chance. Her long-term plan is to become a full-time private nutritional counselor. She is already building a reputation among doctors who refer patients to her. "As your reputation grows, your client base grows," she says.

Growing Public Interest

The field of nutrition is changing, says Elisabeth. "Clients are more health conscious. And cooks are more nutritionally aware, revising their recipes." Like most nutritionists, she believes that people need to reduce the fat in their diets and concentrate on fresh foods, especially fruits and

Dietitians versus Nutritionists

Technically, there is no difference between a dietitian and a nutritionist. In practice, however, the term dietitian usually refers to someone working in a hospital, nursing home, or other clinical setting. In private practice and in the food science industry, most people use the term nutritionist.

There are two paths to becoming a registered nutritionist. The usual route is to attend a college that offers a major in human nutrition with an internship. Graduates must then pass a written examination given by the American Dietetic Association. The second route is to complete a college degree in a related field (such as chemistry), take additional courses in nutrition, then spend a year working in a community program in nutrition. Students then take the national exam.

vegetables. She expects that this focus on wellness and prevention of disease through nutrition will change the future job market. Instead of working only in hospitals and nursing homes, nutritionists will be employed by the government, by corporations and schools, and by health clubs and day care centers.

Elisabeth thinks that in the future fewer nutritionists will have full-time jobs. Instead, she predicts nutritionists will be hired as consultants to corporations or hospitals. They will work on a contract basis, providing services over a period of time for a certain sum of money. Some will be self-employed, with their own practice.

Elisabeth has some advice if you're interested in nutrition and food service: "Read books. And evaluate how you eat. Look at the food in your cupboard and see what nutritional value is in it," she says. "You've got to realize that nutrition is a science."

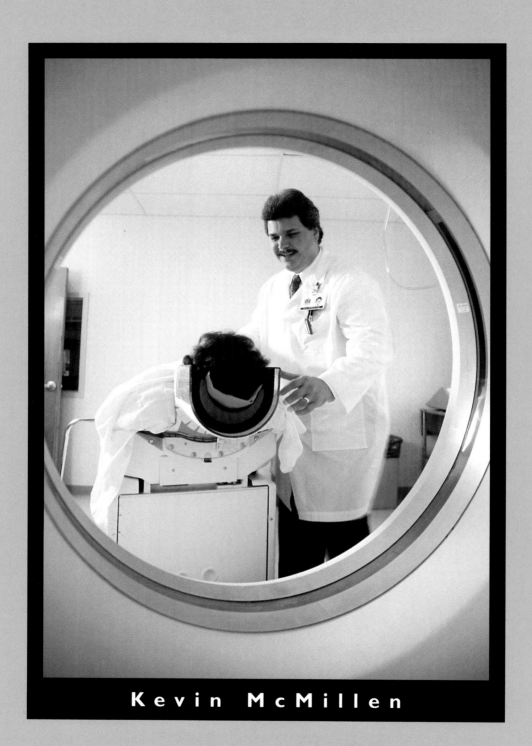

Kevin McMillen

Chapter Ten

RADIOLOGIC TECHNOLOGIST

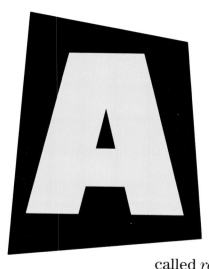

few decades ago, somebody doing Kevin McMillen's job probably would have been called an X ray technician. But his job title is certified medical radiologic technologist. (*Radiologic* refers to the energy produced by radiation. The photographic images of X rays are called *radiographs*.)

"It's a whole lot more than operating machinery," Kevin says. He also helps patients overcome the fear of unknown procedures. "Most patients are grateful for the assistance," he says. And they tell him so, sometimes in person, sometimes in letters and cards. It makes his day.

Kevin began his career at Sinai Hospital in Baltimore when he was still a student. Today he is the team leader for Specialized Imaging, a unit within the Radiology Department. He and his staff of 12 technologists do the high-tech procedures that doctors use to diagnose diseases and injuries. Kevin's specialty is computerized tomography (CT) scans.

Kevin McMillen

CT scans take pictures of the body in layers, like slices of a loaf of bread. Each slice is a separate image. "Together the slices form a 3D image," says Kevin.

Doctors order CT scans in order to see details of soft tissues such as the liver, spleen, and brain. Conventional X rays can be used to diagnose broken bones.

Specialized Imaging

Kevin gets in at 7:00 A.M. to open his unit. He checks the equipment, boots up the computers, and reviews the day's workload. If patients have had previous CT scans, he will request those from the film library. Before patients arrive, around 7:30, he also tries to do a few administrative chores: ordering supplies and reviewing new products.

With Sinai Hospital's two CT scanners, Kevin and his staff can see 25 to 30 patients a day. Each CT scan takes a half hour to 45 minutes, depending on the procedure. "Most of the work of a technologist is at the operating console," he says, "operating the computer during the CT procedures." He sits outside the room that holds the scanner and watches the patient through a window with a video camera.

The scanner is a metal cylinder shaped like a doughnut, with a bed inside. A microphone inside allows Kevin to talk with his patient. On the computer screen he can see the images the scanner takes. He manipulates the images so he gets a complete view of an area. Later the scanned images are converted to X ray film.

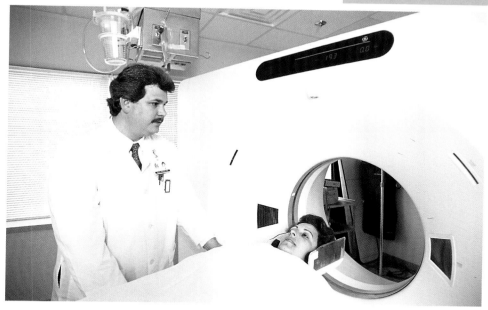

Kevin guides a patient into the CT scanner. Then, on the computer, he monitors the scans of the woman's brain.

Because Kevin is a supervisor, he spends only 30 to 40 percent of his time each day with patients. During the rest of the day, he prepares the budget and payroll, schedules and distributes work to his staff, writes job evaluations, and trains new employees.

There are also meetings with staff and department heads. "The efficiency of our department depends on the efficiency of other services, like patient transportation and nursing," he says. "We work as a team. It's frustrating when patient care is delayed." When his unit is busy, he is often pulled between patient care and supervisory duties.

By 4:30 or 5:00 P.M., Kevin is done for the day. Until recently, he was on call five to seven days a month. Now technologists rotate their hours. By working in shifts, they can provide care 24 hours a day, 7 days a week. Nights and weekends—with car accident and gun shot victims—are often the busiest.

A Hospital-Based Program

When Kevin was young, he found himself in the hospital having an X ray for a broken toe. Already interested in science and math, he told his guidance counselor about the X ray. An aptitude test showed that he was suited for a career as a radiologic technologist.

Kevin entered the 24-month hospital-based program at Sinai the summer after high school. His course work included science—physics, anatomy, and physiology—and professional procedures—radiographic photography, darkroom processing, patient care, and medical ethics. In addition, he did clinical work, producing radiographs under supervision. During these two years, he rotated to a variety of departments, including the emergency room and the general diagnostic department. Later he worked in the operating room, taking X rays during surgery to help the surgeon see what still needed to be done.

After graduation, Kevin passed the comprehensive written national exam to become a registered technologist. Sinai Hospital then offered him a job as a portable/operating room technologist. For a year and a half, he lugged his heavy equipment to wherever he was needed in the

" I like this link between health care and the computer. "

hospital. When he was transferred to the General Radiologic Department, he took X rays for six and a half years.

Then CT scans came along. "It was a completely different diagnostic tool," Kevin says. He learned how to operate the scanners on the job and has worked in the CT Department since 1985. "I like this link between health care and the computer," he says.

Kevin has no interest in becoming manager of the Radiologic Department. "It would remove me from patient care," he says. "You also need a high level of administrative knowledge." He does plan to learn how to perform Magnetic Resonance Imaging (MRI). An MRI is another type of computerized diagnostic scan.

Kevin McMillen

The Art of Communication

For those interested in a career as a radiologic technologist, Kevin believes there are two important traits: an aptitude for technology and a desire to take care of another human being. "Patients who are here often do not feel well and find it difficult to cooperate," he says. "They need your help and understanding. The biggest thing is taking the time to communicate with them. They can be emotional, but seldom do I run into someone who absolutely refuses to do the procedure."

As for the future, "I don't think radiology will go away," Kevin says. But his predictions

Kevin examines a series of radiographs from a CT scan.

aren't completely optimistic. He believes that as hospitals downsize, there may be less demand for X ray technologists.

He expects the technology will continue to change and improve. New types of diagnostic scanners are already on the horizon. Kevin regularly takes training courses and attends conferences to keep up-to-date. If you are interested in radiologic technology, he suggests you take courses in computers, sciences, and math in high school, and do volunteer work in a hospital.

Paperwork

"Paperwork takes me away from my patients."
—Dirk Le Flore, R.N.
"The paperwork shuffle gets confusing and frustrating."
—Karin Tobin, substance abuse counselor
"Paperwork is the worst."
—Michele Rohosky, acupuncturist

Health care professionals are drowning in paperwork. Why is there so much? There are two main reasons. First, records must be kept of every patient visit, complaint, diagnosis, and treatment, including all drugs and therapies. That's because a patient's medical history gives clues to conditions and diseases. The written record also lets teams of health professionals—nurses, doctors, acupuncturists, chiropractors, physical and occupational therapists, pharmacists, nutritionists, and radiologic technicians, to name some—treat the patient together. Good medical records also prevent duplication of treatments or prescribing two or more drugs that, used together, might cause harm.

The second big reason for all the paperwork is the complicated American system of health insurance. Each insurance plan—and there are hundreds, in addition to government plans such as Medicare—pays for different treatments and drugs. One insurance plan might cover chiropractic care, for example, while another might not. One insurance company might pay 80 percent of those expenses, while a different company might pay only 50 percent. And each insurance company uses different forms. Doctors, dentists, pharmacists, hospitals, and sometimes patients must properly complete all these forms in order to be paid.

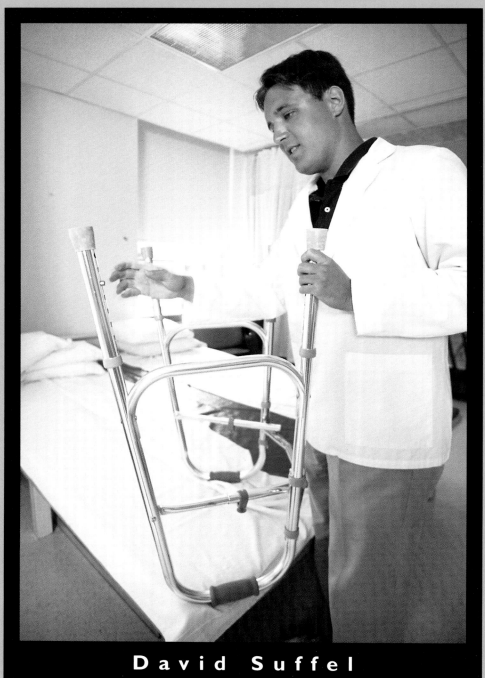

David Suffel

Chapter Eleven

PHYSICAL THERAPIST

hysical therapy is a very diverse field," says David Suffel. A physical therapist might teach a stroke patient to walk and get in and out of bed when one side of his body does not work. Another physical therapist will help an athlete recover from a sports injury by showing her the proper way to train or exercise. Some physical therapists help elderly patients learn to walk after they've had hip replacement surgery. Others might teach people with missing limbs how to use artificial limbs and other prosthetic devices. Despite the many kinds of jobs a physical therapist is trained to do, the goal is always the same: to help patients live independently and return to their normal activities.

David works with the both surgical and medical patients in an "acute" care department of a large hospital. "Physical therapy is a natural fit for me. I really like helping people get well," he says. Having an outgoing personality is a big plus, he believes. "You must tell patients a little progress is good and be understanding when they don't do so well."

He also emphasizes the importance of working with other therapists, doctors, nurses, and dietitians. "You have to communicate—in writing and verbally."

Although David enjoyed science in high school, he didn't want to spend years in medical school. That made physical therapy appealing. It also didn't hurt that PT (as people in the field call it) is a growing field, with high job security and salaries and a variety of workplaces. After graduation from college, David received a number of job offers. "I can do a lot of different things," he says. "It's fun and challenging. There's something new every day."

A Hectic Day

David's workday at an inner-city hospital in Baltimore begins at 8:00 A.M. with a meeting of the health care team. Some mornings he attends continuing education lectures or organizes his schedule. For each patient, he must write an evaluation of the person's condition and a treatment plan with long- and short-term goals. "The paperwork gets to be a little much," he says.

By 9:00 A.M., he is ready to see patients, 8 to 12 each day. He treats most patients in their rooms, although he also works in the gym to take advantage of the whirlpool, stationary bikes, and weights. For new patients referred by doctors, he first does a physical therapy assessment. By palpating, or touching, the patient's body with his hands and observing how a patient moves, he can determine muscle strength, range of motion, balance, and the ability to transfer from bed to chair.

During a typical treatment session, David talks with the patient and checks vital signs and general appearance. He might get the patient out of bed to walk a little, then help

David helps people with injuries or diseases learn to move without pain.

the person move to a chair. "We teach patients how to properly and safely do the activities of daily living," he says. Some of his patients have had strokes and heart attacks, others are recovering from surgery, and still others have been in accidents.

Between treatment sessions, David may teach patients how to use crutches, wheelchairs, or walkers. "Some days I get swamped," he says. "I don't like the overflow of patients and scheduling difficulties."

Since David works with the sickest patients, he sees them for only a week or two, then refers them to another physical therapist for long-term care. Patients range in age, but most are over 60. "It's interesting working with people that age," he says. "They want to get back home and be independent."

If you want to be in the health field, you can't have a weak stomach.

His other patients are admitted through the emergency room. Because David treats people who are HIV positive, he takes precautions against the AIDS virus by using protective gloves. Doctors also refer people with brain injuries to David for physical therapy. They may become verbally and physically abusive. "It's part of the injury," David says.

He also occasionally treats people with wounds or burns. "It's nasty stuff, with infected wounds and blood," he says. "But if you want to be in the health field, you can't have a weak stomach."

David keeps open the last half hour before his day ends at 4:30 P.M. to do billing and finish any paperwork on his desk. He works Monday through Friday, plus a half day one Saturday a month.

An Early Start

Growing up, David often accompanied his father, also a physical therapist, on home care visits. David later volunteered at a local hospital. "I took patients in wheelchairs or stretchers to the rehabilitation gym," he says. Soon he was helping patients with their exercises, under the supervision of a physical therapist. He studied science in high school and made sure he kept up his grades. With fewer than 100 PT programs (for both bachelor's and master's degrees) in the country, the competition for admission is tough.

David earned his degree in physical therapy from the University of Maryland, Eastern Shore. The first three years were filled with science and liberal arts courses. The last two years included professional training. That training included "gross anatomy": dissecting a cadaver. "It's kind of a shock, working on someone who is dead, but it's not as bad as you think," says David. "If you know about the body, you can figure out how things work." In other classes, students learned about special equipment and patient procedures. "It's a pretty intense two years," he says.

David Suffel

To graduate, he also completed several internships. "You are paired with a therapist," he says, "but you're basically doing it." During his training, he worked in an outpatient clinic (where patients do not stay overnight), several hospitals, a home for disabled kids, a public school, a nursing home, and a cardiac rehabilitation unit. "I saw a little bit of everything," he says.

To become licensed to practice in Maryland, David passed a national written exam after he graduated. Other states require clinical tests plus the written exam.

An Aging Population

"Physical therapy will always be around," David believes. "People are getting older. And more active people are bound to have more injuries."

He notes several trends. Corporations are hiring physical therapists to help injured workers ease back into their jobs and stay free from pain or further injury. Physical therapists also work with athletes who are recovering from injuries. David predicts that physical therapy treatment techniques will continue to change and improve. Finally, he expects that future physical therapists will need to earn a master's degree.

If you are interested in PT, "science courses are inevitable," says David. "And talk with people in the profession. Find out what it's really like." Since many physical therapy programs require 30 to 40 hours of volunteer

Like many health care workers, physical therapists must be licensed to practice.

Occupational Therapists

Occupational therapists (OTs) help people with physical and mental disabilities to cope with the tasks of daily life. They teach everything from the most basic skills—dressing and eating—to job skills such as word processing. Many work in teams with physical therapists, doctors, and nurses. OTs must either earn a bachelor's degree in occupational therapy or complete a 14- to 24-month professional course after earning a degree in another field. To become registered and licensed—which is required by most states—OTs must pass a written national exam.

OTs work in hospitals, clinics, corporations, nursing homes, schools, and as home health care professionals. Salaries vary with experience.

experience, volunteering at a hospital is a good way to get started.

As for David's future, he plans to stay at his present job to gain experience in several areas. His next rotation will be on "inpatient rehab," treating people who need additional therapy before they can go home. In the future, he may choose to work full time with a private company to provide home care. "The options are endless," he says.

S u s a n V a n B e n s c h o t e n

Chapter Twelve

PSYCHOLOGIST

sychologist Susan Van Benschoten wants to know why women who were abused as children are more likely to be raped and physically harmed as adults than women who weren't abused. She believes finding an answer to that question is the first step to finding a way to help them.

Susan is finishing a year's fellowship as a psychologist at Baltimore's Shepherd Pratt Hospital. People come from all over the country to Shepherd Pratt for intensive treatment. Most stay for a month. She works with patients who have suffered terrible traumas. Some have been raped or held hostage. Many of the women she counsels experienced severe sexual and physical abuse in childhood. They may experience nightmares or flashbacks to these events. Living in a constant state of anxiety, they have difficulty holding jobs and may even be suicidal.

Why are there so few male patients in her unit? "Men who have been abused often become aggressive and end up in jail," she says.

Susan begins her day at 8:00 A.M. by asking the nursing staff for an update about her three or four patients. Then she attends a community meeting with staff members and patients. Patients have the opportunity to speak out about their concerns. "We let them know someone is listening," Susan says. "We encourage patients to talk to each other directly."

Susan meets individually with each of her patients several times a week. She spends many hours each day in therapy (counseling) sessions. "They need to talk about their traumas in a safe environment," she says. She also helps her patients find practical ways to begin to lead normal lives. Therapy sessions can be funny or depressing or emotional.

Besides her inpatients (the people who are hospitalized), Susan also counsels six outpatients one to three times a week. For each of her patients, she must write a treatment plan and make notes for insurance companies.

After a break for lunch, Susan leads a group on "safety and acceptance" twice a week. "We teach people that it is healing and important to talk about what has hurt them," she says. "It's the purpose of our unit." Once a week, she fits in a meeting with a senior psychologist or psychiatrist to discuss problems she may be having with her patients. She also occasionally tests patients. Rorschach inkblots, sentence completion tests, and pictures help her evaluate patients so she can plan and direct their therapy. She makes her recommendations in a written report.

Psychotherapy, also called therapy or counseling, treats emotional and mental disorders by encouraging patients to talk about their problems.

Susan's day ends around 6:00 P.M. But sometimes a crisis arises. "With emergencies the day gets crowded," she says. "It makes things kind of a mess. I try to beat a crisis, to predict it, and work on it before it becomes an emergency." She carries a beeper for extreme emergencies, such as a suicide attempt.

Susan tries to get away on weekends to hike and horseback ride. "The emotional

We teach people that it is healing and important to talk about what has hurt them.

drain is hard," she says. And although she loves to write and do research, she hates the routine paperwork.

What keeps her going? "It's the patients. I ask: how did this person land in my office?" she says. "I lead with my heart but I also stop and look at things as a scientist." She's often excited by the progress she sees during an hour-long session with a patient.

Abraham Lincoln's Doctor

Susan comes from a long line of doctors, including Abraham Lincoln's physician. The daughter of a naval officer, she attended 17 schools around the country

Susan Van Benschoten

before graduating from high school in Connecticut. She then completed a three-year hospital nursing program in Florida and worked in a series of jobs as an ER nurse. "I liked the fast pace, the intensity of the crisis situations," she says. "It's most challenging working with the human beings behind the injuries and diseases."

Eventually Susan burned out. "I had one too many kids die on me," she says. Yearning for calm, she became a gardener at a residential hospital for 25 young adults in Connecticut. Most of them were unable to function in society. She taught them to grow tomatoes. "These were the throwaway patients," she recalls. "Nobody expected them to get well, but they thrived." Soon she accepted a position as a psychiatric nurse at the hospital, assisting the

Paperwork is an unavoidable part of a career in health care.

psychologist with evaluations and conducting group therapy sessions.

Susan also went back to school, first getting a master of education degree from Antioch College in nearby Massachusetts, then a Ph.D. in psychology at Georgia State University. She did an internship at Pennsylvania State University. "I loved it. For the first time, I had my own caseload and my own clients and patients."

When her current job as a postdoctoral fellow in the department of psychology at Shepherd Pratt Hospital opened, she moved to Baltimore. Unfortunately, her job has been eliminated because of budget cuts. "It's a one-year fellowship," she says. "I wish I could stay." Susan plans to move to Philadelphia, where she hopes to find a job working with abuse survivors. Unlike many psychologists, she's not interested in having her own private practice. "Hospitals are my setting," she explains. "This is where I love to work. I enjoy working as part of the team."

A *fellowship* is similar to an internship—it is a paid position in which the "fellow" continues advanced study or research.

Honesty and Humor

A career in mental health requires adaptability and a willingness to give. Susan believes honesty and a sense of humor are also important. "I don't know what I'd do if I wasn't able to laugh," she says.

To be a licensed clinical psychologist, you need a doctorate (Ph.D.) in psychology. However, a master's degree in psychology or social work, plus experience, may qualify you to work as a therapist. Most states require a number of years of experience as a

Susan Van Benschoten

prerequisite to taking the written exam given by the American Psychological Association.

If you are interested in a career as a psychologist, it helps to know what to expect. Susan suggests becoming a camp counselor or a hospital volunteer—anything working with people. "And get a psychologist to talk to your school classes," she says. Another idea is to volunteer for a school-based peer counseling program.

Mental Health Careers

Psychologists, psychiatrists, psychiatric social workers, psychiatric nurses, and guidance counselors all work in the broad field of mental health. Susan is a *psychologist,* a profession that requires a doctorate in psychology, an internship, and, in many states, a license to practice.

Psychiatrists are medical doctors (M.D.'s) who have done a residency in psychiatry. They are the only mental health professionals who can prescribe drugs. Psychiatrists often treat patients with illnesses such as depression, which is caused by a biological problem.

Psychiatric social workers complete a college degree in social work with a specialization in clinical counseling. They often focus on family issues. In addition, *school guidance counselors* and *school nurses* are trained to counsel students who need help.

Psychiatrists, psychologists, and psychiatric social workers are employed by hospitals, schools, nursing homes, corporations, the military, police departments, and government agencies. Many have private practices. Requirements for licenses vary by profession and by state. Salaries range from high for psychiatrists to considerably less for psychiatric social workers.

To Continue Exploring . . .

Acupuncture

Acupuncture Research Institute
313 W. Andrix Street
Monterey Park, CA 91754
(213) 722-7353

American Acupuncture Association
4262 Kissena Boulevard
Flushing, NY 11355
(718) 886-4431

American Association for Acupuncture and
  Oriental Medicine
433 Front Street
Catasauqua, PA 18032-2506
(610) 266-1433

Chiropractic Care

American Chiropractic Association
1701 Clarendon Boulevard
Arlington, VA 22209
(703) 276-8800

Council on Chiropractic Education
7975 N. Hayden Road, Suite A-210
Scottsdale, AZ 85258-3246
(602) 443-8877

International Chiropractors Association
1110 N. Glebe Road, Suite 1000
Arlington, VA 22201
(703) 528-5000

Chiropractic Technique Magazine
Williams & Wilkins
351 W. Camden Street
Baltimore, MD 21201
(410) 528-4068

Dentistry

American Dental Association
211 E. Chicago Avenue
Chicago, IL 60611
(312) 440-2686

American Dental Hygienists' Association
444 N. Michigan Avenue, Suite 3400
Chicago, IL 60611
(312) 440-8930
1-800-243-ADHA

National Association of Dental Assistants
900 S. Washington Street, Suite G-13
Falls Church, VA 22046
(703) 237-8616

National Dental Association
5506 Connecticut Avenue N.W., Suite 24
Washington, DC 20015
(202) 244-7555

Emergency Medicine

Emergency Medicine Foundation
P.O. Box 619911
Dallas, TX 75261-9911
(214) 550-0911

Emergency Nurses Association
216 Higgins Road
Park Ridge, IL 60068
(708) 698-9400

National Association of Emergency
  Medical Technicians
102 W. Leake Street
Clinton, MS 39056
(601) 924-7744

National Registry of Emergency
  Medical Technicians
P.O. Box 29233
Columbus, OH 43229
(614) 888-4484

Hospital Care

American Association of Healthcare
  Consultants
11208 Waples Mill Road, Suite 109
Fairfax, VA 22030
(703) 691-AAHC

American College of Healthcare Executives
One N. Franklin, Suite 1700
Chicago, IL 60606-3491
(312) 424-2800

American Hospital Association
One N. Franklin
Chicago, IL 60606
(312) 422-3000

Medicine

American Medical Association
515 N. State Street
Chicago, IL 60610
(312) 464-5000

Health Resources and Services
  Administration
Health Services Corps Scholarship Program
4350 East-West Highway, 10th Floor
Bethesda, MD 20814
(800) 221-9393

Mental Health

American Mental Health Counselors
  Association
5999 Stevenson Avenue
Alexandria, VA 22304-3300
(703) 823-9800

National Mental Health Association
1021 Prince Street
Alexandria, VA 22314-2971
(703) 684-7722

Nursing

American Nurses Association
600 Maryland Avenue S.W., Suite 100 West
Washington, DC 20024-2571
(202) 651-7000

National Federation of Licensed
  Practical Nurses
1418 Aversboro Road
Garner, NC 27529-4547
(919) 779-0046

National League for Nursing
350 Hudson Street, 4th floor
New York, NY 10014
(212) 989-9393

Nutrition

American College of Nutrition
301 E. 17th Street
New York, NY 10003
(212) 777-1037

American Dietetic Association
216 W. Jackson Boulevard, Suite 800
Chicago, IL 60606
(312) 899-0040

American Society for Clinical Nutrition
9650 Rockville Pike
Bethesda, MD 20814-3998
(301) 530-7110

Physical/Occupational Therapy

American Occupational Therapy Association
4720 Montgomery Lane
P.O. Box 31220
Bethesda, MD 20824-1220
(301) 652-2682

American Physical Therapy Association
1111 N. Fairfax Street
Alexandria, VA 22314
(703) 684-2782

Advance for Occupational Therapists
Merion Publications, Inc.
650 Park Avenue W.
King of Prussia, PA 19406-1434
(610) 265-7812

Pharmaceuticals

American Pharmaceutical Association
2215 Constitution Avenue N.W.
Washington, DC 20037
(202) 628-4410

Psychology

American Psychological Association
750 First Street N.E.
Washington, DC 20002-4242
(202) 336-5500

International Council of Psychologists
S.W. Texas State University
Psych Department
San Marcos, TX 78666-4601

Radiology

American Registry of Radiologic
  Technologists
1255 Northland Drive
St. Paul, MN 55120
(612) 687-0048

The American Society of Radiologic
  Technologists
  (publishes *Radiologic Technology*)
15000 Central Avenue S.E.
Albuquerque, NM 87123-3917
(505) 298-4500

Substance Abuse

National Association of Alcoholism and
  Drug Abuse Counselors
1911 N. Fort Myer Drive, Suite 900
Arlington, VA 22209
(703) 741-7686

National Treatment Corsortium for
  Alcohol & Other Drugs
444 N. Capital Street N.W., Suite 200
Washington, DC 20001
(202) 434-4780

Alcoholism & Drug Abuse Weekly
Manisses Communications Group, Inc.
P.O. Box 9758
Providence, RI 02940-9758
(401) 831-6020

INDEX

ABOUT THE AUTHOR

Barbara Lee is the author of *Death in Still Waters: A Chesapeake Bay Mystery*, which won St. Martin's Press' 1994 Best First Malice Domestic Mystery Novel Contest. A New Yorker, she now lives in Maryland.

ACKNOWLEDGMENTS

The photographs in this book are reproduced courtesy of: John Danicic Jr., p. 59; Patricia Drentea / IPS, p. 82; © Mark E. Gibson / Visuals Unlimited, p. 98; Andy King, pp. 2, 6, 8, 10, 11, 12, 14, 18, 19, 20, 23, 25, 28, 30, 32, 36, 39, 41, 43, 44, 47, 49, 50, 52, 55, 57, 60, 63, 65, 66, 68, 70, 71, 73, 76, 79, 81, 84, 87, 89, 90, 92, 95, 96, 100, 103, 104; New Jersey Division of Travel and Tourism, p. 78; Dr. Steven R. Pohlhaus, p. 34; Puerto Rico Federal Affairs Administration, p. 54; Science VU / Visuals Unlimited, p. 40; Dr. Frank Sero, p. 33; Jim Simondet / IPS, pp. 16, 17.